12 Step Guide to Overcoming "Whiteness" Without Trying to Be "Black"

by Jonathan Arons

I0440082

Jonathan Arons is a Grammy winning New York City trombonist who has backed up such artists as Aretha Franklin, Alicia Keys, Bon Jovi, and many others as a member of the world renowned Chops Horns (www.chopshorns.com). Jazz credits include playing with the Dave Holland Big Band on the 2005 Grammy winning album *Overtime*. In Salsa/Merengue, he has played with Cuco Valoy and Hector Tricoche. But Arons is most known as the "dancing trombonist", having appeared on various television shows playing a little trombone and doing a lot of dancing. These television appearances, which have become popular YouTube clips, include *America's Got Talent: Season 3*, *Steve Harvey's Big Time*, and *The Tonight Show with Jay Leno*. He has degrees in Jazz Performance and Biochemistry from Oberlin College. In addition, he is involved with his parents' school The Melody Arons Center for Applied Preschool Research. For contact information, visit www.dancingtrombone.com (Photo by Dr. Raymond Arons)

Table of Contents

Introduction

This guide was originally Chapter 15 of a larger book called *Uncle Tim's Condo: What Silly Dancing White Men Represent in Modern Society*. Of all the other chapters I felt this one could stand by itself, as well as test for a potential audience for the complete book. The purpose of this guide is to offer an alternative to many books out there that discuss "whiteness" in popular culture. Books like "Stuff White People Like" (Lander) and "Stupid White Men" (Moore) are either meant to be humorous or self-deprecating in the name of political correctness. This guide is meant to positively confront and overcome the taboo issues that come with having a "white" identity. These issues include:

1. Dancing/performing well to black influenced, popular music.
2. Sincere (soulful) expression in multicultural settings while maintaining an honest individual identity.
3. General behavioral rigidity associated with a white establishment.

As a professional musician and dancer who has freelanced in New York City for thirteen years, I grew tired of the white stereotypes seen in media. I found the white role models for acceptable dancing to black popular music - Hip Hop, R&B, Disco, Funk, House, and the like - to be too extreme. They are hyper athletic, dressed down b-boy white guys from poor neighborhoods standing on their heads in movies like *Step Up (2006)*. Or they are awkward white nerds having little to no physical coordination or sincerity, such as *Napoleon Dynamite* (2004) and *Saturday Night Live* parodies featuring Andy Samberg and Jason Sudeikis. Similarly, politically correct tokenism in popular crime dramas and sitcoms make it so that race issues are either ignored, or comically drawn out as fatalistic faux pas, i.e. the "Larry David moments" in *Curb Your Enthusiasm* and *Seinfeld*.

The only serious race discussions found are usually on news talk shows. Experts there are often passionate people of color or self-deprecating white guys, neither giving convincing reasons for less liberal white people to step outside of their comfort zones. So the questions remain. How does a white person, who is neither super athletic nor a nerd, relate to popular music and multicultural situations? Can there be a moderate ideology for navigating a hyper-politically correct and uptight world? The answer lies within something I have witnessed throughout my career when performing at corporate parties, weddings, and barmitzvahs. A wide range of white people, from the most conservatively privileged to the most liberally rebellious, express desires to dance better to African American influenced popular music. I believe it is this desire to be less "white" that holds some universal answers for solving polarizing identity issues like race.

Instead of focusing on the classic race/class issues like institutional and financial privilege, this guide is meant to focus on how to overcome the expressive disadvantages associated with whiteness. Different *people of all colors* have said to me at various times in my career that they felt "too white" to dance or perform the way I do. They often follow up with the suggestion that I must have some "black" in me. My DNA ancestry tests confirm, however, I am Russian, Polish, German, Irish and English.

The 12 steps presented in this guide are methods I have internalized over the years. They have made it possible to comfortably fit in multicultural situations that intimidate many white people, especially when confronted by black influenced music and emotional vitriol. These steps have helped me dance "black" in front of Steve Harvey on his television show, dance flamboyantly in front of millions on *America's Got Talent*, and perform salsa as Darth Vader in front of elderly Latinos at a Bronx senior center. (These videos are on YouTube, under "dancing trombonist".) And through it all I have maintained my self- respecting, straight white male identity. When discussing racial and class equality, it is the "feeling" entitlement issue that often seems to be missing. My hope is that by presenting ways to develop equal soul power, people will be more inspired to help others with both financial and institutional equity.

Media and the Schadenfreude Paradox

"If you stick a knife in my back nine inches and pull it out six inches, there's no progress. If you pull it all the way out, that's not progress. The progress is healing the wound that the...blow made. And they haven't even begun to pull the knife out much less try to...heal the wound. They won't even admit the knife is there."
- Malcolm X in 1964 interview

In the immortal words of Bruce Lee, "Knowing is not enough. We must act." Self-knowledge and an awareness of power dynamics are useless if we do not apply them. The title of this booklet implies that there is an interest in how to overcome "whiteness." Yes, many would rather embrace their whiteness than overcome it, and this guide is not for them. As the Malcolm X quote says, it is not enough to recognize that race problems exist. While we may have recognized the knife of racism, and other isms, throughout history, the knife must be taken out *and* the wounds healed in the present. This guide is intended as a step forward in that healing. In order to have an integrated society, healing must involve those that wield and are perceived to wield the knife.

Before introducing the 12-step program, let's clarify what I mean by "whiteness". Both *behavioral* and *physical* whiteness is defined in the following table, and can act on a sliding scale within all races, classes, cultures, and social contexts.

Table 1

Physical "Whiteness"	Behavioral "Whiteness"
1. Looking "clean cut", shaved, dressed in a suit or conservative dress and in preppy or expensive clothes.	1. An innocence, ignorance, or denial that race and identity tensions exist in society
2. If NOT clean cut, having straight, long, Jesus-looking hair or straight thin hair styled into "dreadlocks" with a beard and/or long sideburns (if you're a guy).	2. Feeling and acting awkward and self-conscious around racial and cultural minorities.
3. Having European gene pool, no epicanthic fold in the eye, pale to tan skin color, straight skinny nose, straight or curly hair but NOT "tightly coiled" Afro curly.	3. Being physically uncoordinated and unable to express or feel rhythm, usually in the African-American and Latino tradition.
4. Wearing glasses	4. Speaking with proper American English grammar and syntax, with a conservative use of colloquial and cultural slang.
	5. Being overly apologetic, overly expressive of white guilt, or excessively familiar with a minority's experience, which can come off as patronizing and pretentious.

The greatest hypocrisy associated with "whiteness" is reliance on the Golden Rule, "Do unto others as they would do to you" philosophies, while taking self-preservation action. Whiteness has historically involved being two-faced about race. When one politically correct ideal is *said*, but actions are opposite, hypocrisy occurs. Examples in American history include the use of Christianity to justify black slavery. Laws like Jim Crow and the Dred Scott decision were justified because they were enacted in the best interests of everyone, including black people. Today, white people's subtle grabbing of valuables when in the presence of "minorities" demonstrate a Darwinian "survival of the fittest" mentality. These same people may say in the abstract that they are in favor of civil rights, Golden Rule ideologies, but do not make the personal changes necessary to make equity a reality.

I am not immune to the survival of the fittest hypocrisy. For example, despite having enjoyed dating black, Latin, and Asian girls, and being supportive of interracial relationships in general, I sometimes get jealous when I see a black guy (or any other minority) with a pretty white girl. I have to take a moment to check myself, asking if I am defensive because of being white *or* if my reaction is just because I am looking for an excuse as to why that girl isn't with *me*. Because white girls are my color, I find myself offended that whiteness in male form is not good enough for them, all the while knowing that I'm really talking about their rejection of ME. Blaming race in this case seems to be more about hiding my personal insecurities than having to do with protecting those who share my skin color. When a group shares the same insecurities and has power over others, racism and other isms occur. In my case, however, why would I want to fight for a group in which I also feel like an outsider? Am I stupid enough to choose color over character?

When available, race seems to be the easiest explanation of jealousy or envy, because it is visible and the most obvious physical difference. People's most obvious differences naturally justify how they can be threats. It can be much harder to recognize and admit to the non-physical, invisible differences that make someone more attractive (or threatening) - personality, intelligence, life experience, talent and temperament.

We all try to say the right things about race. White people must try harder to say the right things because our skin color and other symbols are historically associated with oppression. Yet for both white and black, joy is often experienced from others' misfortunes, what is called "*schadenfreude"* (pronounced shah-den-froy-deh). It is a key element in comedy and cracking jokes. We experience it during racial jokes usually made in *private*. Enjoying simila*r* jokes about class, however, is much more *publically* acceptable. Hence *class* (behavior) "schadenfreude" is more politically correct than *race* (physicality) "schadenfreude." In other words, when people who look differently from us because of genetics, it is bad to feel good about their shortcomings. If they *behave* differently from us, however, rejoicing in their misfortunes is fine. For example, we rejoice when "the rich" stumble and fall, as we rejoice in having fewer problems than "poorer" people. We often forget that, like our physical bodies, people have little control over the behaviors and cultural experiences they are born into.

In both types of schadenfreude we miss the connection between symbols of class *and* symbols of race, especially in the current climate of political correctness. It is the schadenfreude paradox. We hypocritically enjoy our individual schadenfreude when it comes to the black and white issues of class, but ignore how they apply to race. We make great efforts to ignore these deep contradictions during politically sensitive and cultural situations. We almost never call out the pretentiousness of the nearly all white African drum circles at liberal colleges and the Occupy Wall Street movements. Similarly, we rarely call out black politicians who, once elected, do little to help the poor and middle class people of color like them.

This schadenfreude sentiment is echoed in *South Park*'s episode "1%" (11/2/11). Cartman relates to the 1% in the Occupy movement as a greedy, mean, obese white kid who fails the national fitness exam, bringing his 4th grade's average down to failing so that the school loses funding. He finds fault in the physical fitness exam itself, which is promoted by President Obama. He says three revealing half-truths in the following dialogue. "Wanna know why you're all out here protesting? Because you're pissed off, but you actually think it's wrong to be pissed off at a black president, so you're all just pissed off at me (the 1%)! "

Later he tries to escape a mob by hiding out at Token's, the upper-middle class black students', house. Cartman explains his reasoning: "In this day and age, black people are just impervious from being fucked with, so we will be all right. Token, please! You're the only person I can trust. Because in today's time, black people are somehow incapable of doing anything wrong." When someone suggests that Cartman frame Token for all his crimes, he explains why it wouldn't work: "Nobody would possibly blame Token for all of this, because in today's day and age you can't blame a black person for anything."

What is Cartman really saying here? Among other things, *South Park* seems to capture the sentiment that society is reluctant to criticize upper and middle class minorities who achieve high office or status in business and media. If they have weathered public relation storms to hold onto their money, and maintain their pop cultural relevance, they have proven themselves as white and mainstream friendly. Two dynamics result. One, it becomes a boy who cries wolf scenario. Any new type of criticism, valid or not, can be written off as racist because of white guilt and America's history of racism. Two, it goes back to the commonly held assertion that no matter how rich you are, if you have "darker skin" color you will always be black. No matter how rich or how much material power Obama, or any other minority politician has, trusting him to be on the side of the less fortunate 99% of Americans is easy because his relative darker, "black" skin. The concept of "black" continues to be tied to the symbolism of angst and the less fortunate. Obama's symbols of blackness, more visual than auditory, are invaluable for distracting the masses if he actually chose to govern in the interests of the primarily white 1%. Even so, many disenfranchised poor and middle class blacks are not "impervious from being fucked with". Just ask those in poor urban neighborhoods that police constantly harass to reach their arrest and fine quotas.[1]

It is difficult to explain this schaudenfreude paradox because we are accustomed to talking about racial and class issues only in material terms. Alternately, we discuss *feelings* only when it comes to

---

[1] "The NYPD Tapes: Inside Bed Stuy's 81st Precinct," *The Village Voice*, 5/4/10

art and music, often ignoring the material circumstances that led to the original creativity. We talk about ideologies only when it comes to politics and religion, ignoring the emotional and material circumstances that inspired their sets of rules. In order to constructively confront today's problems and get inside the motivations behind society's polarized divisions, we must consider all factors. It is not just the money in politics, but the various ideologies and social rituals that contribute to our political games.

Martin Luther King Jr.'s quote, "I have a dream that my four little children will one day live in a nation where they will not be judged by the color of their skin, but by the content of their character" is thrown around like handy-wipes whenever a sound bite is needed to promote some sense of political correctness and divisional tolerance. Unfortunately, his quote seems to continue to encourage ignorance about how symbols of character and symbols of color continue to be connected. Arguably, we see "race", just as we judge character, based on visual symbols of dress, style, facial expressions, and personal hygiene. We just do not want to admit it.

Advertising is an area where we refuse to consciously recognize how color and character are linked. For example, a P-Diddy advertisement for his clothing line, Sean John, features a young, dark-skinned black boy, fist in the air, signifying the black power pose black athletes made in the 1968 Olympics. The advertisement uses the words, "a new look, a new fit, a new day." It is ironic that the advertisement says "new look" when the pose is 60's black. Within today's context, however, the look of color is linked to a different type of character. Color, the black race of the boy in the ad and P-Diddy, is linked to the mainstream character of fashionable rebellion. But it is not enough to put your fist in the air. You must buy the clothes to attain that justifiable angst, coolness, and swagger. Movement and action are not enough to define such character. Material clothes do. P-Diddy's adverts seem to say, "If you cannot be black, buy my clothes, and you can have as much black swagger and angst as you want and still be rich".

Calvin Klein and other white fashion designers use mostly white models, looks, and poses to cater to the conservative white buyer. "The NEW look, fit, and day" belongs to the black person and other people of color's commercialized angst. As a white man who does not feel comfortable in the look of a conservative white person, hipster, nerd, or the apologetic man-child, I should not feel pressured to buy and look "black" to justify my own angst, rhythmic feel, and style. Of course it would be easier to turn a blind eye, imagining that since P-Diddy is black, he only has the best intentions for my differently oppressed white soul.

The opposite of schadenfreude is envy and vicarious enjoyment. There is enough envy to go around on both sides of white and black. People envy things associated with stereotypically "white" elite material status: easier access to food, shelter, clothing, and opportunities for physical comforts, objects, and free time. People also envy things associated with stereotypically "black" soulful sensual status: drive, justified chips on the shoulder, angst, physical prowess, and passion in music and other expressive art forms.

In a world blinded by political correctness, ignorance of how we connect color with character affects what we buy, what we feel entitled to say, and what paths we choose in life. The following 12 steps on "how to overcome whiteness without trying to be black" are written with the "white" musician and dancer in mind. The information in these steps, however, much like the information in Zen books for archery and motorcycle maintenance, may be applied to other people in similarly polarized situations.

One of my favorite quotes from Bruce Lee's *Enter the Dragon (1973)* is when a fighter tries to intimidate Lee, asking him about his style. Lee replies "My style? You can call it the art of fighting without fighting." Lee ends up getting the best of his adversary without laying a finger on him. The following 12 steps are presented to get the artist, the creative person, the participant in any multiracial or multicultural ritual, into a headspace that liberates the soul to express itself on its own terms. I believe the key, as described in the first step, is to be fully aware of your own symbols in relation to those in the immediate environment. This way, you can start defining yourself based on your own flavor and brand of physically having, feeling, and believing.

I would like to present a method of being politically real, current, and cool as a white person without relying on the examples of a ranting liberal pundit on MSNBC, a self-deprecating John Stewart on Comedy Central, or an uptight white guy on FOX. I believe any talking head, white or black, that does not include themselves in the discussion of class or race, and only points to other sources of those issues, is a phony. Where are the serious discussions, not jokes, about "soul" and the many different factors contributing to our individual and collective ideologies?

I want to present a way to be rhythmic and soulful, without the need to imitate Eminem, Timberlake, or Bieber. I do not trust any "white hope" in music who has not fully disclosed how they deal with the race issue, the same issue that I believe has kept music from

14

making greater progressive innovations. It is the same issue that prevents most white people from participating in dance and other social rituals that are multiracial and multicultural. It seems that a white guy can only be taken seriously in dance if he stands frozen, upside down on one hand, or does a choreographed ballroom partner dance. By the end of the 12 steps, any soulfully challenged person will learn how to get respect by doing a simple side to side step in rhythm. Like Bruce Lee's method, this can be viewed as "dancing without dancing" so that we do not have to become a caricature of something we are not, nor a joke of whom we really are.

Step 1 – "Overcoming the Tim" Oath

Step 1 is meant to diffuse the white guilt with people of color and other minorities that gets in the way of participating in dance, conversation, and a variety of cultural rituals as soulful equals. What often happens is a defense mechanism of making an offensive excessively familiar statement, or purposefully dancing silly, soulfully submissive, and clueless. These are all traits of what I call an "Uncle *Tim*" character. I have an oath to recite that reconciles material privilege with an equal entitlement to seriously urgent expression. Without recognizing the material privilege associated with your whiteness, it is practically impossible to claim a stake in soulful equality. After reciting this oath as a white person, you will no longer feel compelled to make fun of your whiteness, feel awkward around minorities, or belittle your own experience to compensate for elephants in the room. You will immediately get more respect for taking responsibility for your white symbols and what they represent. Nobody will catch you off guard again by playing a race card to belittle your opinions or expressive efforts. This is your first step toward being able to confidently share and learn from people who are different from you. This way we can become a more united human race and better fulfill our individual potentials for greatness. Recite the following 3 part oath:

A.) Despite whatever my ancestral history is as a white person, I have benefited from the system built on cheap labor provided by black people and minorities in this country. It is not enough to proclaim that times have changed and this country is the land of opportunity and unlimited possibilities. It is not enough to simply declare that this great country offers equal opportunities for everyone to exercise their free will. As a white person, none of that is enough to cleanse and wash away centuries of oppression and genocide. My white guilt can only be purged by admitting that I have received many benefits I would not have if I did not have white skin. The sins of people who looked like me before my lifetime paved the way for much of the privilege I receive now. (Admit it. Admit it fully. Recognize the weight and gravity of such a statement.)

B.) I recognize that I did not have a choice in the body I was born into nor was anyone else given choices for theirs.

C.) As someone who has benefited from this body in this place, I promise to help others who do not have the same symbols and environments that have benefited me. By participating in these actions, I am exempt from being part of the destructive past by being part of a different and greater future. I am born again as a soulful equal as long as my actions reflect these intentions.

Step 2 - Clapping on Two and Four

The next few steps are about participating in musical rituals that are stereotypically difficult for white people. In most rock, jazz, R&B, and hip-hop music, one can hear the drums accent beats 2 and 4 in a song with four beats per measure. In other words, unless a song has 3 beats, such as a waltz, most popular songs in American culture are in sets of 4 beats, the 2nd and 4th beat accented more than the 1st and 3rd. Did you ever wonder why white people give you a funny look when you clap on 2 and 4 to pop songs? You might even be too scared to clap along, but all you need is practice and experience. Clapping on 2 and 4 is often done in black churches, where so much of our popular music has its roots. Many people who are raised in the black church develop abilities to participate and hear popular music this way.

I believe clapping on 2 and 4 is an essential way to both affirm your American heritage and give credit to black culture. Since so much of popular music has these black rhythmic elements, learning how to consistently clap on 2 and 4 can be a valuable asset for acceptance in multicultural rituals. But practice first in private. Tap along with your favorite pop song, making sure it has 4 beats. Feel the pulse. Initially count the beats over and over again in your mind, 1, 2, 3, 4. Every time you count "2" and "4", listen to the drums and clap your hands with them. You can also *walk* while counting out loud or in your head. I find there is no better method to find a steady rhythm than walking at a steady pace. Most people take a walk at one speed, especially in the middle of a longer walk. During those walks, clap every second and fourth step. Make sure that your hand claps at the same time your foot lands on the ground.

If you want to really work on your popular music feel, go to a black church on Sunday and clap along with everyone else. Practicing in large groups, especially as a joyful, communal activity, makes clapping on 2 and 4 feel more natural and helps you relate more confidently to the live experience of listening to bands and performing artists who invoke this feel in clubs and other public events.

A steady beat is essential in order to relate to any of this. Not everyone has rhythm. But I guarantee that more white people have rhythm than they give themselves credit for. After getting the "2 and 4" beats down, try clapping the clave in Latin music. Ask your knowledgeable Latin friends and they will tell you about the clave. With each rhythmic experience, notice how you expand your rhythmic abilities beyond your white identity.

Step 3 - Bopping Head

Do you remember the 2002 Will Smith song, "Black Suits Comin' (Nod Ya Head)"? Everyone in the video nods their head downward to each beat. Don't do that. At least not in this exercise. That is the "white" way. The black actor/rapper Smith made this song in a white way to cater to his large white fan base, similar to later years when he was a foil to Kevin James' white spastic dancing in the movie, *Hitch*. Much of white-rock-oriented-music demands this downbeat head action because that is where the rhythm is rigidly emphasized. Heavy metal and hard rock head-bangers are prime examples. But the point of these 12 steps is to break out of the comfortable habits associated with whiteness, to broaden our horizons and be comfortable in a world increasingly defined by color, black R&B, dance, and hip-hop. The next time you listen to some hip-hop, R&B, dance infused music, try bopping your head in the opposite direction on the downbeat. Move the head **back** as if you're looking up to where the wall meets the ceiling on every pulse in the music. Your head will "nod" back downwards during a funkier upbeat, making it ready to bop backwards again for the next pulse. In fact, the act of bringing your head down affirmatively on the upbeats naturally strengthens your feeling for the syncopation found in much of the popular "black" music today.

Don't get me wrong. Headbanging is cool. But bopping your head backward will encourage you to feel music differently from the usual white tradition. These exercises are about transcending your origin and reaching beyond white comfort zones. While it is important to recognize and give credit to origin, the ultimate purpose of these exercises is to build soulful bridges based on mutually empowering interests. That does not mean you have to act like something you are not. You share experiences based on feeling from the inside-out, instead of material ones from the outside-in, an essential for improved cross divisional exchange. Your feeling of new sensations helps to overcome whiteness, as opposed to simply buying different clothes and appropriating a few words.

Step 4 - The Two-Step (Side to Side)

Now that we have basic principles about moving our hands and head to popular American music, we must address the feet. I like to think of a famous Zimbabwean proverb for Step 4: "If you can walk you can dance. If you can talk you can sing." I'm going to let you in on a little secret that may be pretty obvious to some. All my dance moves that have gotten me on so many television shows are just extensions of one dance step – going side to side and repeat.

When taking beginner dance classes, I found it interesting that many students were enthusiastic about learning various styles - hip-hop, funk, locking, street-jazz or house - and yet seemed to have difficulty simply stepping side to side in rhythm during class warm-ups. I never understood how anyone could expect to learn a stylized dance move, with complicated arms and footwork, without knowing the basics. It is not just knowing the basic side-to-side move, but also about enjoying it naturally to your favorite music. Everything starts with the two-step. If you cannot do a two-step with joy, confidence, and conviction, don't even try to learn another dance move. Most white people at the events, parties, and weddings where I perform get so caught up in trying to imitate me that they lose the rhythm of the two-step on which all my movements are based. If you want to overcome "whiteness" on the dance floor, feel free to be silly only after you can be serious.

The two-step can be done to any music that is counted in sets of 4 or 8 beats. Disco, house, and most pop music with 85-120 beats per minute are good choices for practicing this step. Contact me or ask friends for song suggestions if you cannot find any simple dance disco/house/hip-hop/club songs that have these characteristics. Like the Zimbabwean proverb implies, the energy of the step should have a walking aspect to it. There is no need to step especially high or wide. Simply start with your feet together side by side. On beat 1, step your right foot to the side. On beat 2, move your left foot to join the right foot so that they are together. On beat 3, take your left foot again and step to the left. On beat 4, step your right foot to meet your left foot. Repeat the process. That is the two-step.

In the beginning, do not add arm movements. Too much arm movement can be distracting. Forced arm movements can lead to frustration with the footwork. It stirs up demons in your head about looking silly like the character Carlton from Will Smith's television show *The Fresh Prince of Bel Air*, and Rick Astley's "Ric Rolling". You'll want to stop because you can't take yourself seriously. Keep all the rhythm in your feet at first. If you must do something with your arms, just slightly bend them at the elbows as if you were going jogging.

Find joy in moving side to side. Own it. Once stepping side to side becomes natural, put your personality into it and add simple arm movements. You will be amazed how many compliments you get as a white person for being able to move from side to side in rhythm. People will want to dance with you. If you are a male, you will score major points with both girls and guys for your basic rhythmic groove.

Once you get this down, consider taking a basic dance class with Brian "Footwork" Green, or Raymond "Spex" Abew, both great NYC choreographers and dance teachers. They teach a great exercise on developing your own style, which takes a little more coordination. While your feet keep the general tempo going side to side, try making your head move according to what other instruments you hear in the song. Perhaps your head moves according to where the bass drum accents. Then second, make your arms move another way to a different instrument's rhythm, maybe the guitar. The key is to listen to the song, to connect to the different instruments complimenting each other, and to be in the moment. You become one with the song, surrendering your body. By the end of the exercise, three different parts of your body are holding down different, yet compatible rhythms to the same song. That can be a bit advanced. So first just work on going side to side and remember. OWN IT!

Step 5 - "Go White Boy!"

At this point, you might have tried the last three exercises and felt silly or self-conscious. Be patient. If you can picture yourself being capable, you can have rhythm. Practicing at home helps. Applying what you practice to the outside world is more challenging. If you do not apply your rhythmic practice to real life situations, it is like going to church on Sunday without being a good Christian during the week.

It is natural to feel self-conscious around clapping, two-stepping, and head bopping people if you are a new to participating instead of just watching. When self-conscious, there might be a desire to overcompensate for your nerves. This may translate into an over-enthusiasm to get it right, or the exact opposite - a shutting down of all feelings or apathy. The spontaneous joy gets lost when you are overly enthusiastic or apathetic due to fear and self-consciousness. Without joy, there is no rhythm. Be cool and wary if you feel yourself overly enthusiastic or shut down in front of other people. Remember why you love music, even if you have to be still for a moment to compose yourself. Let the rhythm hit you. Feel it. Be inspired and try reacting to it with the basic soulful expressions of clapping on 2 and 4, two-stepping, and bopping your head.

Never force the feeling. Forcing a feeling is a common "white" tendency when relating to black music and other multicultural situations. Trying anything new can feel forced at first. Be patient. Trust these exercises by taking it slow, even if that means moving and clapping to slower songs. What makes the two-step and the other basic physical exercises come to life is the emotional content, your attitude and personality. Self-consciousness comes out in attitude and rhythm. I find *joy*, *passion*, and *anger* to be the most inspirational emotions for being rhythmic. Silliness and humor can also be effective, just as long as they are not defense mechanisms for feeling insecure. Guilt, however, is a rhythm killer. Let it go.

If someone calls you out on your race, realize you are much greater than the category they are trying to put you in. I found that the reasons people have called me out as a "white boy," "cracker," etc., is to make me feel bad about something I cannot change, my skin color and what it represents. How can white people compare the history of the "n word" with the derogatory ones having to do with "whiteness"? Often the white derogatory terms of white boy, cracker, peckerwood, etc., are most intimidating when involving expressions of rhythm and physical prowess. The advice I give to myself and to others, who sometimes feel marginalized by these "white cat calls", is to take a page out of the book of so many black people who deal with the n-word. I advocate transcending the spoken and written word by acting in ways outside of how white boyishness and "crackerdom" are defined. Many black people throughout history have transcended the offensive identities associated with the "n word" by cultivating their minds and bodies. If we truly believe in human equality, white people must have the same discipline to cultivate their rhythm, their minds, and their bodies to become equally *innovative* and soulful contributors to American music and pop culture.

Just as many black people have learned from white people throughout American history, white people need to be more comfortable learning from black teachers. To be clear, anybody good enough in any field can teach anyone else. I know that feeling when people doubt a student's ability to learn and a teacher's ability to teach because on their culture or race, instead of their knowledge and talent. Just as so many people of color have grinned and born it, overcoming the hurdles of white institutions, don't let the sarcastic "go white boy" deter you. Know who you are. Take unshakable pride in your life experience. Remember that your love for music is more powerful than any physical difference that separates you from the people who originally created it. You are as much a descendant of the first Africans as are Americans of color.

Once you remember your birthright as a human being, entitled to all things material, sensual and unconditional, consider the source calling you names. It is likely that the person calling you out on "whiteness" is caught up in a material world where white skin represents more of a threat than who you are individually. Realize the context of the source, understand it, forgive it, and let it go. Just because they are self-conscious of their material state does not mean that you have to become self-conscious of yours. Let your sensual and creative state consume you, the one expressing its glory and greatness through rhythm.

Step 6 – "Color" Visualization

This exercise is something I find myself doing in the New York City subway from time to time. I first got the idea in college. Back then, some of my college musician friends and I joked about how the Puerto Rican leader of the salsa band we played in looked a lot like Gregory Hines, only he was lighter-skinned. Of course, many Latin people have black African heritage, so it is not unusual for some to look "black." But consider this. A few years ago, a friend of a girlfriend told me that I looked like Wayne Brady, the dark-skinned comedian/actor! I was flattered because Brady has always been an idol of mine, but I wasn't sure what she meant because I'm pretty pale white. She went on to say that we have similar smiles. I started thinking that we had similar shaped mouths and jaws and roundish faces. About a year after that, I noticed that a very dark-skinned black girl on the subway had similar looking eyes to the Asian girl next to her.

Those three incidents made me think about how fluid racial identity can be. There have been times when I thought that a person looked like a white, Asian, or Latino version of a black guy, or a black, Asian, or Latino version of a white person. Sometimes it's not about looks. People can be described as *acting* like their racial version of a person from another race. As politically incorrect as it sounds, I thought about actively looking at people and imagining what they would look like if they came from another race. I'm not just talking about imagining someone darker or lighter-skinned. I mean imagine what each individual would look like with every different racial characteristic. Aside from different colors, imagine what a person would look like with a wider or thinner nose, different eyes, and with curly, afro-ish, and straight hair. Picture it as a comparable exercise to the one recommended for speaking in public – the one where you imagine your audience naked. But instead of nakedness, you imagine changing physical nuances of the people you see around you. Picture a computer like the one the teenagers use in the movie *Weird Science* (1985). Instead of just tweaking body parts of a woman, you tweak everything on everyone you know inside your head. When picturing your friends looking different, can you picture them acting the same? While picturing strangers in the street as different races, would you assume different things about them? It takes some practice, but once you do this type of visualization, it is amazing how many more similarities you might notice between so called different races. This helps you to become less self-conscious about what race you are in multicultural situations.

Along the same lines, a great skill to develop is reading body language. Paul Ekman, a famous scientist, wrote a book titled *Emotions Revealed.* It explains the facial muscles that form expressions, from the very subtle to more obvious, and which reveal what people actually think and feel. Especially in today's world, we get caught up making behavioral judgments based on dialects, accents, and colors instead of the universal human expressions visible in body language, particularly the face. Ekman's years of fieldwork reveal that all "races" of humanity express emotions – from happiness to sadness – in the same facial way. While it is necessary to recognize differences according to our different genetics and cultures, it would be easier to do if we understood that we universally express similar emotions in our faces, enabling better communication and fewer assumptions. The visualizations' exercises in this step, together with Ekman's exercises on recognizing facial expressions, are invaluable for cross-divisional communication.

Step 7 – Group Mind
(For Musicians and Dancers)

Bands are made up of different sections - woodwinds, brass, and percussion. Orchestras have, in addition to these, string sections. Within each section there are more sections. A brass section has separate trumpet, trombone, French horn, euphonium and/or tuba sections. There are often 3 to 5 different parts in each section. In jazz bands and orchestras, there is usually one person per part while in concert and community bands there can be many people playing the same part. Growing up, I've played in huge concert bands with as many as five people on the same part.

When I first started playing I wanted to show I was the best in the trombone section. Regardless of the music markings, I always tried playing the loudest and most correct notes, hoping that the trombonist next to me would get intimidated and make mistakes. I forgot that the point of playing within a trombone section is to sound like one big trombone. Instead, I hoped that the conductor would scold the guy next to me and compliment me. To show that I was the best, I also would rush just a little bit to get the notes out a hair faster than anybody else. I thought playing in a band was like being the first to raise your hand in class. This proved to be a problem. Between not paying attention to the dynamics on the music or the conductor's tempo, my efforts to be the best did the opposite. The conductor would stop the band, my section mates nudging me for rushing and being too loud. In thinking that it was all about me, I missed the point of why playing with other people is so special.

What makes playing in a band special is how everyone complements each other, united by the same rhythm and sense of cooperation. They become greater than the sum of their parts. One of the peculiar and amazing things about playing music in a band is when you play with someone you may hate, all in the name of making good music. You can still be competitive, but it becomes a competition about becoming the best team player, which requires a certain sense of making peace. Music quality diminishes when the main priority is getting the most individual attention.

Having played both ways makes me wonder if other people also rush (play ahead of the beat) when they are overly competitive. Rushing is about a goal. Good music and dancing is about the journey. Maybe people rush to the end of the phrase or, in the case of dancing, get the moves out first to show that they know what is coming, instead of enjoying the journey. Granted, there are people of all races who do not have rhythm. With white people, however, the quality of rushing can be out of a sense of over-enthusiasm and competition. Too much enthusiasm leads to over-thinking things in needing to prove you have skills, which can often lead to rushing and bad rhythmic performance. Trying too hard to groove is not grooving at all.

For those who do have some rhythm but not have enough practice expressing it, the secret is to connect in the moment. Develop trust and a group mind sense with whom you play and dance. Dance groups look better when everybody does choreography at the same time. Bands playing with the same rhythmic intensity sound incredible. A person slightly ahead or behind makes the whole group look bad.

When I feel competitive and under pressure in a dance off, or during a trombone solo, I sometimes rush and fall out of the groove. During those moments I feel really "white." The advice I give myself or anybody else that performs within a group is to let go of your competitive tendencies. When having a solo or competitive moment, it is important to still outwardly connect with your opponent. You have a greater chance for victory with an outward connection and awareness with your environment than the inward disconnected focus that leads to rushing or dragging (slowing down).

There is nothing more rewarding than the give and take that happens within a group united by the same groove. This group mind set doesn't just apply to music, but to sports, acting, and any other group activity. Comedy improv, creating a scene from scratch live in front of an audience, is very big on "group mind". Every actor supports the other actor's suggestions by "yes and-ing." Though my profession is music, there are times that I believe you cannot get more group-minded than when performing comedy improv. I try to apply the skills I learn from improv to music.

If you can overcome needs to rush, get ahead of people, and stand out, the most fun happens when you can get in the zone and mess with timing of a song as a group. Of course, it is important to keep good time, but it is also important to let it breathe a little bit. Laying back behind the beat in a horn section is easier when you can relax and trust each other. Trust also happens more naturally if you know each other outside of an activity. That's why people hang out. People often form groups, musical or otherwise, based on both talent and friendships. When performing with the Chops Horns section, I love how we can lay back playing horn lines a little behind the beat, giving them a funkier feel. Our chemistry is also a testament to the many gigs and hanging out we've done together. A section that clings together, swings together. (OK. That was corny.)

Step 8 - Imitate, Stylize, and Innovate

Perhaps white guilt is partially to blame for why black people made most of the innovations in American music, establishing its original rhythmic and soulful identity. Step 8 discusses actions needed in order to become as much of an imitator, stylist, or innovator in American music as any person of color.

In November of 2011, Nicholas Payton, the famous jazz trumpet player, posted a poem on his blog. He was frustrated with the label of "jazz," its cultural relevance, innovations within it, the business side of giving credit where credit is due, and historians' interpretations of it. It triggered a firestorm of different reactions. Some people said it did not matter what you called it as long as it "swings." Others used it as an opportunity to vent other frustrations about music and identity. The biggest issue for me was who got the credit for innovation.

The most interesting reaction has been to start a movement to rename jazz "BAM," short for Black American Music. Justifications say that "jazz" was originally as derogatory a word as the "n" word, both invented by oppressive white people. The main argument for BAM was to give permanent credit to the black people who originally created the music. Many say that in addition to origin, black people have been responsible for most innovations throughout the evolution of jazz. As soon as Payton and other jazz musicians made that claim, automatic pushback included arguments that there were white people who played as skillfully and contributed to the art form. Payton's response, entitled "An Open Letter to Marcus Strickland and His Facebook Friends", included the following statement:

> I am trying to fight for what Duke Ellington wanted to do for this music years ago, call it Black music. Why? Because he knew back then that if we didn't label it in a way that spoke of its origins, that years later, White folks would try to lay claim to it like it was a collective invention…Don't get me wrong, there are some brilliant, genius White cats that have played this music, but it's ultimately a Black art form. What's wrong with renaming the music in a way that puts that argument to bed once and for all?...Black American Music was created by Blacks, but it belongs to everyone. **BAM!**

Payton is absolutely justified in his position. Still, if a name like "BAM" (Black American Music) is about recognizing origin, it should also include rock, funk, R&B, hip-hop, dance, and all types of popular American music. Why stop at defining "jazz" as Black American music? It is probably because Payton is not a rock, R&B, or Hip Hop artist. Ultimately, the whole BAM issue seems to be an attempt to make jazz (or himself) more relevant to black American youth instead of the primarily nerdy/white/Asian/European/upper-middle class/and college jazz major fan base. By saying, "it belongs to everyone", Payton seems well aware that without this core constituency, jazz primarily only lives on in senior citizens and former 80's and 90's young lions like himself. Maybe his feelings were similar to mine mentioned earlier in the shadenfreude section. Sometimes it is easier to blame race instead of confronting more individual insecurities.

Payton's points also remind me of a discussion about the difference between innovators and stylists in a Jazz History class I once took at Oberlin. Innovators were those who changed the game, who introduced a new technique and way of playing. Stylists were the ones that put their own personality and phrases within the frameworks that innovators established. For example, as far as saxophonists go, Charlie Parker and John Coltrane were innovators. Sonny Rollins, Joe Henderson, and Michael Brecker were stylists. In basketball, Michael Jordan was an innovator while Kobe Bryant and Lebron James are stylists. In computers, Bill Gates, Steve Jobs, and Dennis Ritchie are innovators. Those who make various products, PCs, X-boxes, iPads, are stylists.

Not everyone can be an innovator. That is a wonderful thing. If everyone innovated, there would be no united movements, everyone trying to make their own. Possibilities and personal styles within each innovation would not be explored to the fullest. But before we find a personal style, we start out IMITATING. When studying Jazz in college, we were told to transcribe jazz solos and copy other jazz musicians' phrasing. Learning this way is comparable to imitating our parents' speech, other family members, and friends. Depending on the time in your life, your speech is influenced by all these people to different degrees. From these internalized imitations we make our own expressions.

Because jazz has become increasingly "white" and international over the years, other cultural influences outside of the African American tradition are taking the music to new places. But why is jazz mostly white now? Why can't there be more white people in hip hop/modern R&B etc.? I've developed a theory about White

Gentrification and Black Flight in music. The pattern in America has always been that once enough white people imitate a black innovation in American music, black Americans take flight from that soulful space per se, and move on to innovate something new.

This pattern is enabled by a fear of superior expressive abilities and an envy of passionate angst. In other words, many religions and philosophies talk about how *suffering* grows the *soul*. In the white/black dynamic of American racism, white people have been both threatened and inspired by black people's ability to endure extreme suffering. They are envious of the resulting soul power to innovate expression. As an artistic expression grows distant from its original source, many people will imitate it in memory of and in reference to the original suffering. In the most general sense, such suffering translates into soulful urgencies to procreate, to emote, or be creative in any way. It just becomes a question of whether a person uses the soulful (suffering) expressions of today or yesterday. Jazz, yesterday's cutting edge black protest music, becomes what so many white intellectuals play today. The only black people left to express jazz are cultural conservatives struggling for relevance in the modern world, often settling for classical and academic institutional preservation. So if the current American black/white pattern persists, in 50 years young hip hop artists will be mostly white performing at colleges alongside the likes of old black rappers while black youth will have innovated something else. If white Americans are to *innovate* something as visceral as jazz or Hip Hop in popular music, it will require a uniquely white, intense suffering and universally sympathetic experience.

Sometimes we are intimidated to imitate certain people

because we think they are too black, white, feminine, masculine, technical, or primal. Regardless of how much we admire them, we are afraid to imitate them because we do not look like them. We think we cannot behave or perform like them. The purpose of Step 8 is to say this: NOBODY IS UNIMITABLE. If you like what somebody does, if you wish you could do the same thing, imitate them no matter what it is they do or what they call it. Imitating requires study and focus. To imitate, you have to study slowly to internalize every note, sound, move, and delivery. While getting inside the sound or movement, you find where your soul fits. You find parts of your own experience that inspire you to make sounds and movements as powerful, maybe more powerful, than who originally made them. Once that happens, you have a better chance at innovating and creating something new. Do not let any sound or movement intimidate you. Never feel you are not entitled because the innovator has a different kind of body or lifestyle from you. Sometimes we just like what we like for unconventional and inexplicable reasons.

For example, I stopped singing as a kid mainly because I was afraid of becoming gay, which for me meant being forced into an uncomfortable lifestyle. Deep down, however, I always wanted to sing but thought it was too late. Even now, learning how to sing and write songs as an adult, instead of gay issues, I worry about trying to sound too "wannabe" black. Yet I am envious of the white people who pull it off. Who taught them that that was okay? How did they have the strength to continue imitating even if people around them said they were trying to be black? They probably did so in the same way that I learned how to dance. Maybe dancing was something in which I had more talent and was unwilling to give up, no matter what people called me.

Imitating other instrumentalists is much easier than imitating singers. We are all born with different vocal chords. Now that I am discovering my voice for singing, I beat myself up, wondering what I was scared of. Broadway music stereotypically has very "white" approaches with less "riffing" and improvising than R&B. Maybe my style will be somewhere in between, something I have yet to discover. Ultimately, I wonder if I could be a better singer today if I was as fearless in trying to imitate Marvin Gaye and Ethel Merman, as I am imitating Fred Wesley on trombone, or doing the "wop" and other old school black party dances.

So whether or not jazz ever becomes BAM, I wonder if white *Americans* will ever be solely credited with an innovation in popular American music. Even country music is often called white blues. Whatever that new music would sound and look like, it will only happen if more "white" people shamelessly imitate, personally style, and make that leap to innovate something that changes the game. Let us never forget that innovation can happen in all of our colors, shapes, and experiences.

Step 9 - The Roads Less Traveled

The 9th exercise takes you out of your comfort zone. Everyone develops routines to make their lives easier. We are creatures of habit. We get used to one way of doing things, one group to socialize with. Being white, it is easier to take certain comforts for granted. Aspects of both physical and behavioral whiteness is having enough money to be comfortable, and feeling that you are in the majority of what defines normal. Therefore, experiencing more discomfort, more uncertainty about your place in the world is another way to transcend "whiteness." To be clear, "slumming" does not count nor does going to an expensive club or concert hall to hear multicultural jazz. Serving at a soup kitchen doesn't count unless you actively engage with the homeless and hungry as equals.

What counts is putting yourself in a position where you have equal or inferior status and within a context where you are a minority in some unfamiliar way. It seems very common for white people to use words, music, and phrases taken from other cultures without having experienced any of the culture firsthand. Instead, they learn cultural appropriations from outdated, institutionalized sources, through sanitized video screens, and carefully chosen poster children. Getting used to being an outsider by exposing yourself to people of different classes, languages, and mannerisms for an extended amount of time is essential to adapting to an ever-changing world in which materials and expressions are increasingly borrowed from other cultures.

Consider how "bling bling" was added to the Webster's Dictionary in 2003. "Bling bling," a phrase that originally came from disenfranchised black hip-hop culture, is defined in Webster's as "flashy jewelry that indicates wealth." In my experience, however, I've noticed white people who say "bling bling" generally are just trying to be funny and show what a novelty they are for saying something soulfully black. So many white people used the word as a joke that it became mainstreamed. I would be curious to find out how many of the white people that made "bling bling" popular enough to be put in the dictionary actually said it in front of black people.

How do you get yourself out of your comfort zone? Try incorporating a weekly (or daily) non-life-threatening ritual of putting yourself in unfamiliar social dynamics. Go to a club, restaurant, or even school where you are a minority and submit to the rules of the house. Socialize and have fun interacting with the people there. As a musician, I often find myself in such dynamics, playing at R&B/funk/pop clubs and restaurants in different neighborhoods, playing in salsa bands, and working with the gifted and disabled at my mother's school. I also volunteer at inner city schools, figuring out how to present the trombone, and the music and dance I bring to it, so that it is meaningful to them. It gives me an opportunity to see what they are into and what things are current to them. This in turn helps me know how to share what I know with them. There are many different ways to get out of your comfort zone. The key to overcoming whiteness, however, is the intensity and duration of your outsider experience.

Ultimately, by purposefully putting yourself out of your comfort zone you are better equipped to face adversity when it happens. You are better equipped to communicate ideas beyond your family and friends by exposing yourself to different experiences and different people in both upwardly and downwardly mobile situations. There are times, after all, when we cannot rely on family and friends, and have to find comfort and support elsewhere. The skills to find comfort in the unfamiliar are especially important during times that force us to redefine our selves and our self worth. You connect with people outside of your comfort zone and become comfortable wherever you are.

Step 10 - Beyond the Shackles of Political Correctness

Step 10 is something to keep in mind once you've gotten more experience stepping out of comfort zones. It is one thing to be respectful and say the right things around people who are different from you. It is another to be real. There are many times when I am around minorities that I feel pressure to prove myself as a humble white person who does not make judgments based on race, all while monitoring how I am being judged. I get sick of feeling fake, not allowing myself to show my true emotions. Sometimes when I'm in a bad mood and happen to be performing at a black club, I feel that I have to watch how I express myself. I get scared that my bad mood will come off as racist, even when my mood is unrelated to the black people I'm entertaining.

That may sound crazy and out of line, but it brings me to the next point. It is extremely liberating when you are totally real and take risks expressing yourself "politically incorrectly" around people that are different from you. Some have a hard time being real around people they know, let alone those who are unfamiliar. Something happens though when you are more regularly around people who are different from you. Sometimes you get to a place where you can use their language and phrases without offending them. You get a better sense of when it is appropriate and when to flip it on them to make them laugh or make a deeper emotional connection. There comes a point where you can let your guard down. That is a beautiful place. It can be challenging because ugly things might come out. Some unexpectedly delicious moments can happen, too. When you make mistakes, apologize and learn from them,

Nevertheless, even during apologies, it is essential not to get caught up in being too politically correct. Being too politically correct is like putting up walls that hide your true identity, your true feelings, your true questions. There's a certain acceptable dishonesty about political correctness. At the end of the day, we should be able to communicate openly without the shackles of mincing words. It is a very fine and necessary balance to strike, especially if you are white and privileged. It is a different balance for everyone.

To avoid overly politically correct moments, make sure you have an honest emotional investment with people. Don't enjoy the moment because you are trying to prove something "meta" or abstract, like "ooh look at how multicultural I'm being". Enjoy the moment because you enjoy something within someone that you see in yourself or would like as part of yourself. You can even call those qualities out in the conversation so that your polarized differences do not distract from sharing that deeper admiration. Ultimately, people who are obsessively politically correct are hiding something. They probably have never allowed themselves or been forced to take honest chances outside of their comfort zones. We have to be willing to make mistakes if we want to show and share who we really are.

Step 11 - Admit It
When You Do Not Know

A common mistake I have made as a musician is trying to look smarter than I am. This is not an exclusive quality to whiteness. Still, when white people get caught acting like they know something they do not (especially about black culture), it tends to look that much worse. There have been moments I was so relieved to find acceptance among musicians of color or musicians with higher status, that when they asked me if I'd heard of something I hadn't, I lied and said "It sounds familiar" when I'd never heard of it at all. I worry that if I say, "I don't know. I never heard of them," I will no longer be considered cool enough. I especially feel this way among more successful jazz peers, even though I have a degree in jazz and play with many great jazz musicians. I feel pressured to act like I know what's going on in the jazz world, even though my main interest is in "old skool" R&B and disco. Still, even when around NYC R&B veterans, I get embarrassed about how much I do not know.

Looking back, I kick myself in the head for trying to act like I knew stuff that I didn't care about in order to look cool in front of people who would have little to do with my life's path. It took a long time for me to realize how sick I was of trying to please the jazz gods and establishment, when at the end of the day I'd rather get my groove on to some disco funk, or shamelessly sing a cheesy Broadway standard. I ended up lying to them and myself. When you admit you do not know certain things, you will get to know more quickly who you are and where you fit in. I may not know the latest about who's who in different scenes, but I do know that I'm talented enough to hang with anybody. I know that I can lift the energy in any performance situation. While it is important to know what the current trends are, it is more important to know yourself. Knowing what others are doing is not going to help if you can't produce something of your own. As long as you know yourself, where you come from, admitting what you don't know is okay. Ask someone what he/she is talking about. Who or what is such and such? It's okay. While some people might initially put on an air of surprise and superiority, they will often end up more impressed with your honesty. Admit ignorance so you can learn something new with pride and humility. Then you can decide whether what they say is worthy of *your* time. How about that for empowerment?

Step 12 - Forget Everything and Just Do It

Step 12 is the most basic exercise when applying any type of knowledge. It is also the hardest. Countless philosophers and religious leaders have their own words to describe Step 12. This is my attempt. After repeating all the exercises to develop the muscle memory involved with two-stepping, clapping, and bopping your head, along with the mental skills for expressing yourself in uncomfortable situations, you have to forget all of the training. Living in today's supposedly post-racial, post-modern era, trying to consciously apply these exercises to every social situation can be overwhelming. A voice teacher once said "You're trying too hard to get it right. When you think about trying to get exercises right, they become stagnant. Stagnant is always wrong. Don't be timid. Be spontaneous!" The same goes for any type of expression, whether it is dancing soulfully at a party, or making a formal presentation at a business meeting.

These exercises are meant as vehicles to free you from hang-ups associated with being "white" within a world increasingly influenced by color. They aren't meant to be bubbles of protection and pretension. Whenever you forget how to be your whole self in any context, these exercises can help you find your way. There is nothing like being purely in the moment of an expression, becoming one with rhythm, tonality and everything surrounding it. There is no more race, no more divisive classifications, only body and soul.

www.ingramcontent.com/pod-product-compliance
Lightning Source LLC
Chambersburg PA
CBHW050834290526
45792CB00001B/394